MIKE PIAZZA

BABE HERMAN

SANDY KOUFAX

JOE McGINNITY

ZACK WHEAT

KIRK GIBSON

RAUL MONDESI

DON DRYSDALE

JACKIE ROBINSON

OREL HERSHISER

DAZZY VANCE

DON NEWCOMBE

THE HISTORY OF THE
LOS ANGELES
DODGERS

WAYNE STEWART

CREATIVE C EDUCATION

Published by Creative Education, 123 South Broad Street, Mankato, MN 56001

Creative Education is an imprint of The Creative Company.

Designed by Rita Marshall.

Photographs by AllSport (Jonathan Daniel, Otto Greule Jr., Scott Halleran, Matthew Stockman),

Associated Press/Wide World Photos, Icon Sports Media (John Cordes, David Seelig),

SportsChrome, TimePix (Tony Linck)

Library of Congress Cataloging-in-Publication Data

Stewart, Wayne, 1951- The history of the Los Angeles Dodgers / by Wayne Stewart.

p. cm. — (Baseball)   ISBN 1-58341-212-3

Summary: Highlights players, managers, and memorable games in the history of the

baseball team which began in Brooklyn in 1890 and moved to the West Coast in 1958.

1. Los Angeles Dodgers (Baseball team)—History—

Juvenile literature. [1. Los Angeles Dodgers (Baseball team)—History.

2. Baseball History.] I. Title. II. Baseball (Mankato, Minn.).

GV875.L6 S83 2002   796.357'64'0979494—dc21   2001047867

First Edition 9 8 7 6 5 4 3 2 1

WHEN PEOPLE

THINK OF LOS ANGELES, MANY PICTURE THE GLITZ AND

glamour of southern California and Hollywood. The sprawling city

is famous for its many posh suburbs, including Bel-Air and Beverly

Hills. Home to nearly three and a half million people, the "City

of Angels" has the second-largest population of any city in the

United States.

When baseball fans think of Los Angeles, most picture a

dynamic, winning tradition. The Los Angeles Dodgers are one of the

oldest teams in the game, dating back to 1890 when they joined the

National League (NL) as a team in Brooklyn, New York. Back then,

fans got to the ballpark by darting across Brooklyn's trolley tracks,

trying to avoid being struck. That eventually led local writers to dub

WILLIE KEELER

the team the "Trolley Dodgers," a name that was soon shortened to the Dodgers.

In **1890**, Tom Lovett became the first (and only) Dodgers pitcher to win 30 games in a season.

{WAY BACK WHEN} The Brooklyn Dodgers were a big success from the start. The club won the very first NL pennant in 1890, then claimed two more in 1899 and 1900, before the World Series was created. Two stars of that era were pitcher "Iron Man" Joe McGinnity and outfielder "Wee Willie" Keeler. McGinnity got his nickname because he was so durable he often pitched in both games of a doubleheader. Keeler, who was a mere 5-foot-4 and 140 pounds, was a superb hitter who described his batting approach as simply, "Hit 'em where they ain't."

After its strong start, Brooklyn struggled mightily in the early 1900s. The Dodgers finally made their first World Series appearance in 1916, losing to the Boston Red Sox in five games. Back then, the

RAUL MONDESI

Colorful hurler Clarence "Dazzy" Vance averaged 16 wins a season for Brooklyn.

DAZZY VANCE

team was guided by popular manager Wilbert "Uncle Robbie" Robertson. During his 18-year reign, which began in 1914, the Dodgers remained respectable and took on a new nickname, "the Robins," in his honor.

Outfielder Zack Wheat, who played in more games than any other player in Dodgers history, excelled under Robertson's guidance. In 1918, he led the NL in hitting with a .335 average. A great curveball hitter, Wheat was also outstanding on defense, boasting one of the league's strongest arms. "Zack Wheat," wrote one reporter, "was 165 pounds of scrap iron, rawhide, and guts."

In 1920, pitcher Burleigh Grimes helped the Dodgers capture another NL flag. Grimes was good, but pitcher Clarence "Dazzy" Vance—another Dodgers star of that era—was simply incredible. Vance won more games than any other Brooklyn pitcher in history

A Brooklyn star of the **1920s**, outfielder Zack Wheat batted over .320 for six straight seasons.

ZACK WHEAT

Like former great Zack Wheat, in-fielder Mark Grudzielanek was a high-average hitter.

MARK GRUDZIELANEK

(190), led the NL in victories in 1924 (28), and topped the league in strikeouts for seven consecutive seasons. His numbers were all the more impressive considering he didn't start his major-league career until the age of 31.

A **1939** game between Cincinnati and Brooklyn was the first pro baseball game ever televised.

{BREAKING THE COLOR BARRIER} The Dodgers didn't win any pennants in the 1930s, but they had a lot of fun. Known to fans as the "Daffy Dodgers," the team featured a number of colorful characters. Foremost among them was a poor-fielding outfielder named Babe Herman, who once misjudged a fly ball so badly it hit him on the head. "He wore a glove for one reason," quipped Dodgers second baseman Fresco Thompson. "It was a league custom." Herman made up for his terrible fielding with great hitting, however. In 1930, he set a team record with a stunning .390 batting average.

In 1941, the Dodgers put all silliness aside and won another

PETE REISER

pennant. That season, outfielder Pete Reiser led the NL in batting,

and first baseman Dolf Camilli drilled a league-leading 45 home

runs and was named the NL Most Valuable Player (MVP).

Unfortunately, the powerful New York Yankees emerged victorious

over the Dodgers in the World Series.

During the first half of the 1900s, major league baseball

unofficially banned African-American players from the game. But in 1947, Dodgers president Branch Rickey signed a black infielder

named Jackie Robinson to a big-league contract. Rickey was aware of the controversy the signing would cause, but he believed Robinson was the perfect player to make history. "I'm looking for a ballplayer," Rickey told Robinson, "with enough guts *not* to fight back."

Shortstop Pee Wee Reese showed a sharp eye at the plate in **1947**, leading the league in walks (104).

Robinson faced hostility and jeers from many opponents and fans, but he prevailed. In his first season in Brooklyn, he helped the Dodgers win another pennant, scored 125 runs, and earned the very first NL Rookie of the Year award. Known for his intensity and daring base-running, Robinson would eventually become the first African-American to enter the Baseball Hall of Fame. It was written that the more Robinson was "taunted and threatened, the more he

OREL HERSHISER

let his performance on the field speak for himself."

In 1949, the Dodgers won their third pennant of the decade.

Unfortunately, they also lost their third World Series of the decade,

despite efforts like those of pitcher Don Newcombe, who won the

Rookie of the Year award that season. Seven years later, Newcombe

would win the Cy Young Award and the NL MVP award, making

him the first player to win both awards in one season.

{WINNING IT ALL...FINALLY} The Dodgers won NL

pennants again in 1952 and 1953. Unfortunately, as

had happened in 1941, 1947, and 1949, the team was

then beaten by the New York Yankees in the World

Series. Brooklyn fans continued to believe in their

Dodgers, however, following each heartbreaking

defeat with their famous war cry: "Wait till next year."

In **1949**, the great Jackie Robinson batted .342, stole 37 bases, and was named the NL MVP.

The 1955 season turned out to be the year fans had been

waiting for. That season, Dodgers manager Walter Alston guided

such stars as outfielder Duke Snider and catcher Roy Campanella to

a 98–55 record and Brooklyn's third pennant in four seasons. In the

World Series, it took seven games to knock off the Yankees, but the

waiting was over at last—Brooklyn finally won it all.

Brooklyn fans were jubilant, but they were crushed just two

JACKIE ROBINSON

Gary Sheffield rekindled memories of such slugging Dodgers stars as Duke Snider.

years later. In October 1957, the Dodgers announced that—after 68

seasons in New York—they were moving to Los Angeles. Team

From **1962** to **1966**, Sandy Koufax led the NL in ERA every season (with an average of 1.99).

officials wanted to build a new stadium, but when

New York officials failed to come up with a suitable

site, the Dodgers packed up and headed west.

Los Angeles fans greeted the relocated team

enthusiastically. In 1959, the Dodgers whipped that

enthusiasm into a frenzy by winning another world championship,

topping the Chicago White Sox in the Fall Classic. Pitcher Larry

Sherry led the way, earning two victories in the World Series.

{THE KOUFAX ERA} The Dodgers captured two more World

Series championships in the 1960s, thanks in large part to the efforts

of one player: Sandy Koufax. Perhaps the greatest left-handed pitcher

of all time, Koufax used a devastating curveball and smoking fastball

to lead the Dodgers to three NL pennants during the decade. He

SANDY KOUFAX

also led the league in ERA for five straight seasons.

Koufax was virtually unhittable at times, throwing one

no-hitter each season from 1962 to 1965. Only legendary hurler

Nolan Ryan engineered more no-hitters than Koufax did. The three-

time Cy Young Award winner won 25 games in 1963, then topped

that total with 26 and 27 victories in subsequent seasons. "I can see how he won 25 games," said Yankees catcher Yogi Berra in 1963.

"What I don't understand is how he lost five."

Koufax had a strong supporting cast during the 1960s. He teamed with pitcher Don "Big D" Drysdale to give the Dodgers a fantastic one-two punch. Drysdale, a perennial All-Star, was an intimidating player known to throw more than one pitch in tight

to an opposing batter. "The second one lets the hitter know you meant the first one," said the feisty pitcher.

Speedy shortstop Maury Wills led a Dodgers infield made up entirely of switch hitters during those years. He set a major-league record with 104 stolen bases in 1962 and helped make Los Angeles a daring team on the base paths. The Dodgers of his time loved to bunt, steal, and stretch singles into doubles. "When he runs, it's all downhill," said Dodgers announcer Vin Scully of Wills's speed.

WES PARKER

Power-hitting catcher Mike Piazza made his mark on Dodgers history in the '**90s**.

MIKE PIAZZA

24

The Dodgers had another star in the outfield in the '60s: Tommy Davis, a great hitter who topped the league in batting average in 1962 and 1963. He enjoyed his finest season in 1962, leading the NL with 153 RBI. This loaded roster made the Dodgers a powerhouse throughout the 1960s, bringing home World Series trophies in 1963 and 1965.

Pitcher Don Sutton spent 16 seasons in Los Angeles, winning a franchise-record 233 games.

{NEW FACES, SAME RESULTS} The Dodgers continued to

win in the 1970s, going to the World Series in 1974, 1977, and 1978. Sadly, they were beaten all three times, losing to their old rivals, the Yankees, in the last two appearances. Still, they averaged an impressive 91–70 record each season from 1970 to 1980, largely through power hitting and great pitching. Just as Koufax had sparked the team in the 1960s, hard-throwing pitcher Don Sutton led Los Angeles in the '70s.

DON SUTTON

While Sutton anchored the Dodgers' pitching staff, outfielder Dusty Baker and first baseman Steve Garvey headed up a powerful offense. In 1977, Baker and Garvey teamed with third baseman

Ron Cey and outfielder Reggie Smith to make Los Angeles the first team in baseball history to feature four players who each hit 30 or more home runs in a season.

New faces appeared over the next decade, and so did two more World Series trophies. In 1981, pitcher Fernando Valenzuela was a 20-year-old rookie sensation, posting a 2.48 ERA, becoming the first rookie ever to win the Cy Young Award, and sparking a fan following known as "Fernandomania" in Los Angeles. His heroics and the leadership of manager Tommy Lasorda helped the Dodgers beat the Yankees in the World Series that season.

In perhaps his best season, first baseman Steve Garvey hit 33 homers with 115 RBI in **1977**.

After several disappointing years, another Los Angeles pitcher took center stage during the 1988 season. That pitcher was Orel Hershiser, who set a new big-league record by throwing 59 consecutive scoreless innings—an amazing feat that helped him win the Cy Young Award. "Hershiser may never have another year like 1988," noted one sportswriter. "Maybe nobody ever will."

Outfielder Kirk Gibson also carved his name into Dodgers lore

STEVE GARVEY

in 1988. That season, the Dodgers again reached the World Series, where they faced the Oakland Athletics. Even though Gibson was

Center fielder Brett Butler had a history-making season in **1991**, playing 161 errorless games.

sidelined with a leg injury, he was called on to pinch-hit in game one with Los Angeles behind 4–3 with two outs in the ninth inning. The hobbled star limped to the plate and crushed a home run into the right-field stands to win the game. Four games later, the Dodgers

finished off the A's to capture their sixth world championship.

{THE YO-YO YEARS} The 1990s were a mix of highs and lows for Los Angeles. The Dodgers won the NL Western Division title in 1995 and made the playoffs as a wild card in 1996. However, it was also the first decade since the 1930s that the club didn't make a World Series appearance. In 1992, Los Angeles lost 99 games, a new team record for futility.

Still, the Dodgers did become the first major-league team ever

BRETT BUTLER

to produce five consecutive Rookie of the Year award winners (from 1992 to 1996). That string of young stars included first baseman Eric Karros and heavy-hitting catcher Mike Piazza. Karros hit 20 home runs in his rookie season and went on to become a mainstay of the team's offense. Piazza, meanwhile, spent five full seasons with the Dodgers and shattered numerous team records, including the most home runs by a rookie (35) and the most homers in a season (40). He also hit for the highest batting average of any West Coast Dodgers player ever (.362 in 1997).

Japanese pitcher Hideo Nomo rang up 236 strike-outs in **1995** and was an All-Star Game starter.

Three other stars of the late 1990s were ace pitcher Kevin Brown and outfielders Raul Mondesi and Gary Sheffield. Mondesi became the first Dodgers player to chalk up at least 30 home runs and 30 stolen bases in a season—a feat he accomplished twice. Although Sheffield lacked Mondesi's speed, he was just as powerful

HIDEO NOMO

A tough
veteran, ace
Kevin Brown
won a com-
bined 41
games from
1999 to **2001**.

KEVIN BROWN

Outfielder Shawn Green boasted a rare combination of smarts, speed, and power.

SHAWN GREEN

at the plate. During the 2000 and 2001 seasons, the perennial

All-Star launched a combined 79 home runs and drove in 209 runs.

Los Angeles fans saw a rising star in young short-stop Cesar Izturis, a great defender with speed.

Although Sheffield was traded away in 2002, Los Angeles made up for the loss by bringing in pitcher Hideo Nomo and veteran outfielder Brian Jordan.

Much about the Dodgers franchise has changed over the years. Instead of sidestepping Brooklyn trolleys to get to the ballpark, Dodgers fans today weave through thick traffic on the Los Angeles freeways to reach Dodger Stadium. As the team's 21 NL pennants attest, however, the team's winning ways have remained a constant. As longtime Dodgers manager Tommy Lasorda once said, "The names change, but the Dodgers tradition remains forever."

32

CESAR IZTURIS